SCHIRMER'S LIBRARY
OF MUSICAL CLASSICS

Vol. 149

CARL CZERNY

Op. 337

Forty Daily Exercises

For the Piano

With Prescribed Repetitions
for Acquiring and Preserving Virtuosity

Edited by

G. BUONAMICI

G. SCHIRMER, Inc.

DISTRIBUTED BY

HAL•LEONARD®
CORPORATION
7777 W. BLUEMOUND RD. P.O. BOX 13819 MILWAUKEE, WI 53213

Daily Exercises.
Introduction.

CARL CZERNY. Op. 337.

There is nothing more advantageous and important for one desirous of pursuing any art, than the assiduous practice of all the most oft-recurring difficulties, persevering in this until perfect facility is acquired.

Such is the aim of the present studies; and if the player, after learning them thoroughly, will practise them according to directions and with Maelzel's metronome in the tempo prescribed, his fingers will become capable of executing the most difficult passages with ease.

It will be understood, that the title "Daily Studies" does not imply that all these exercises are to be played through in a single day. On the contrary, about one hour ought to be devoted to the study of a portion of them every day, three or four days being thus required to finish the course; this will be fully sufficient to attain the end proposed.

These studies are to be played with all the repetitions indicated, and without any interruption whatever, in the prescribed tempo; only after each coda a short pause may be made.

Repeat each measure 20 times without interruption.

*) Also transpose a semitone higher, using the same fingering.

Each repeat 20 times without interruption.

13435

4

Allegro. (♩ = 112)

4.

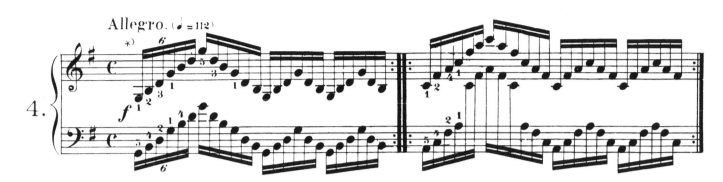

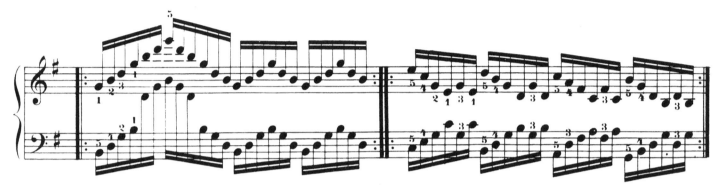

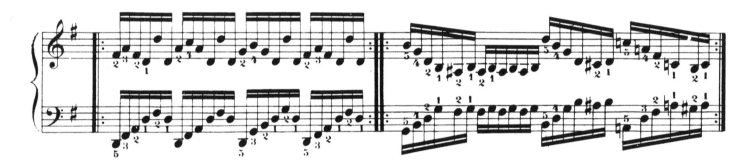

Coda.

*) Also transpose into G♭, without changing the fingering.

13435

Each repeat 20 times.

Allegro. ($\bullet$ = 80)

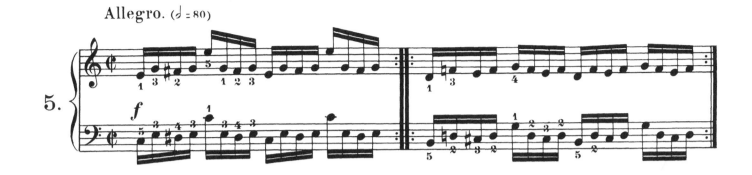

5.

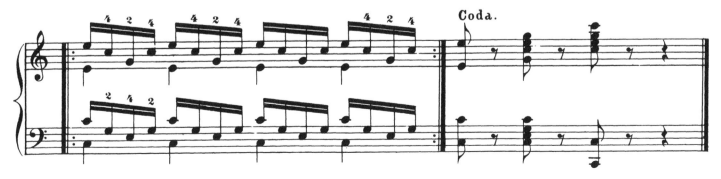

Coda.

6

Each repeat 20 times.

6.

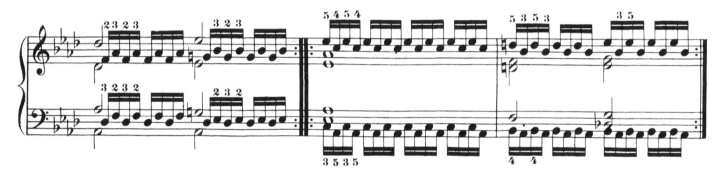

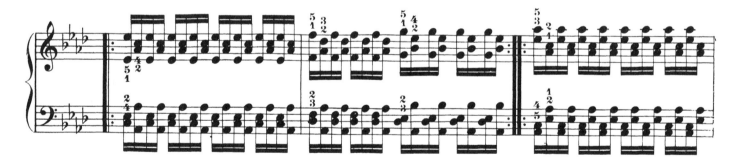

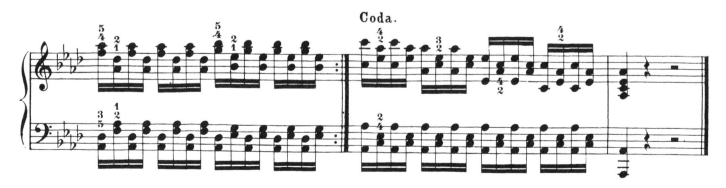

*) Also practise in A major.

13435

Each repeat 10 times.

Allegro. (♩.= 50)

7.

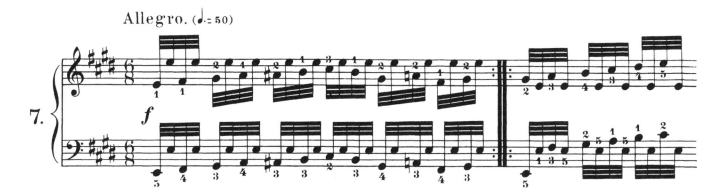

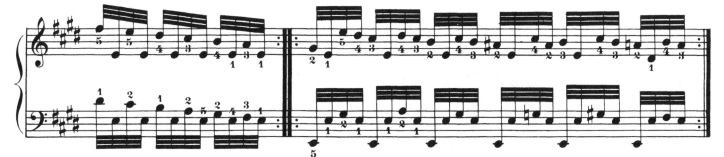

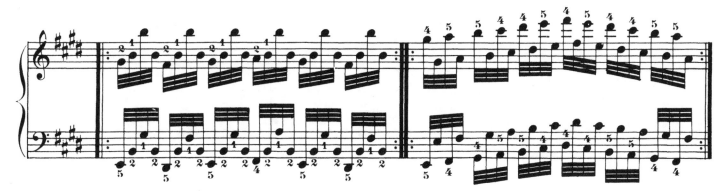

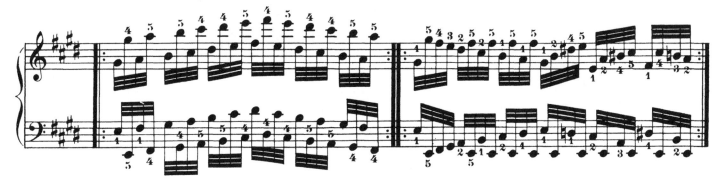

Coda.

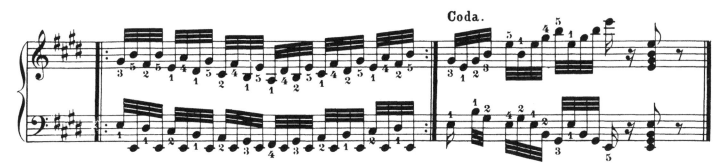

Each repeat 15 times.

13435

Each repeat 30 times.

9.

Each repeat 8 times.

Allegro molto. (♩=104)

10.

Coda.

12

12.

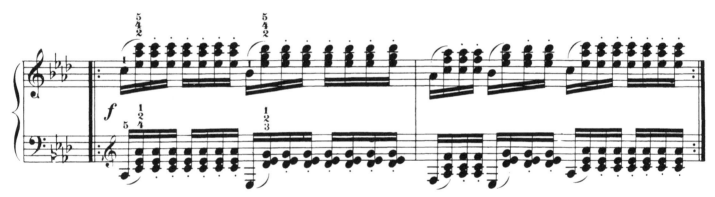

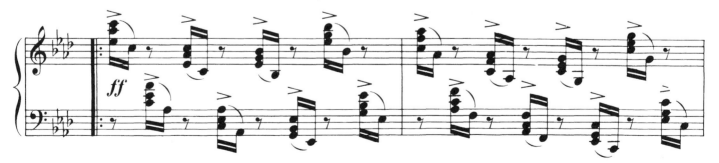

*) Also transpose into A major, making necessary changes in fingering in the last 3 repeats.

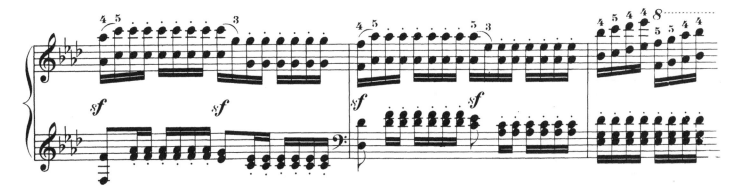

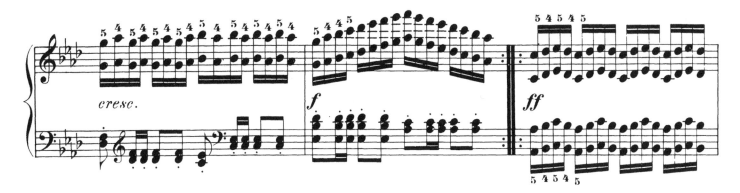

Each repeat 12 times.

13.

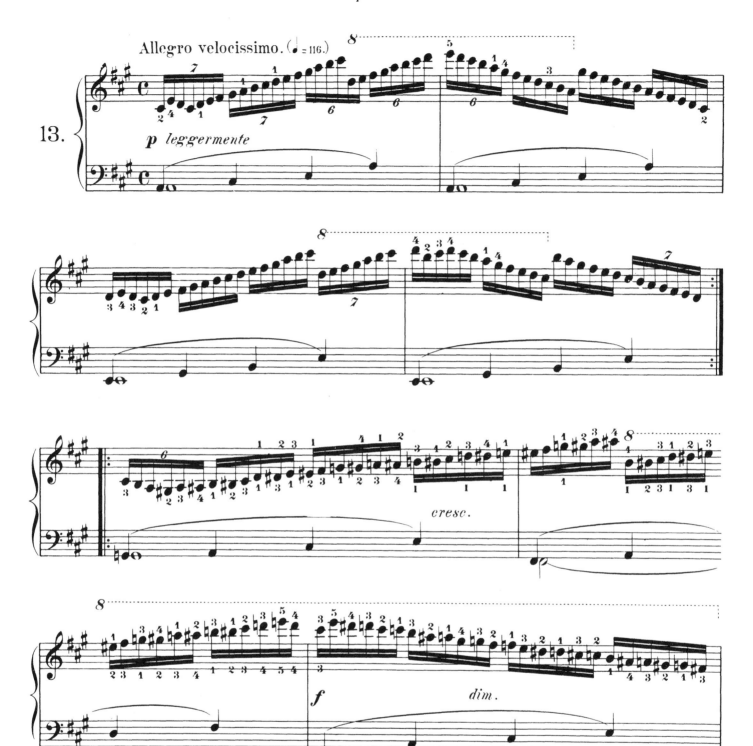

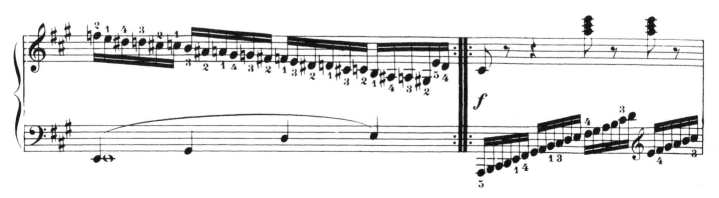

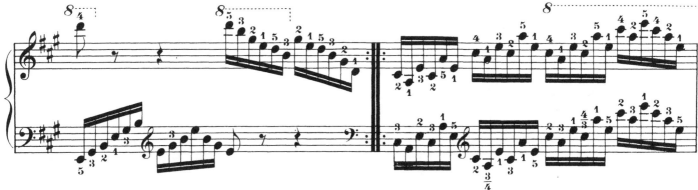

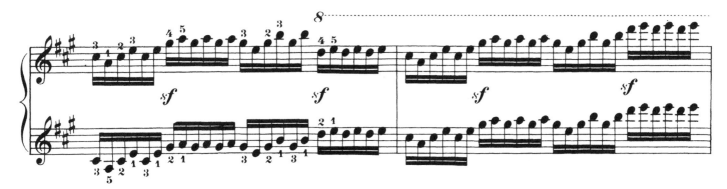

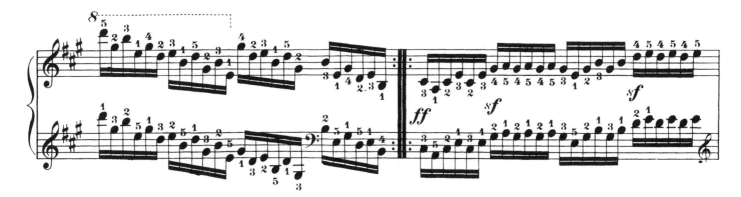

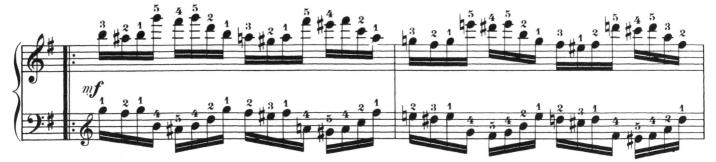

13435

Each repeat **16** times.

Allegro molto. (♩=69.)

16.

p leggermente

cresc.

dim.

f

Coda.

Allegro. (♩.=66.)   Each repeat 8 times.

17.   p stacc.

Coda.

*) Also practise in A major.

Allegro. (♩=92.) Each repeat 6 times.

18.

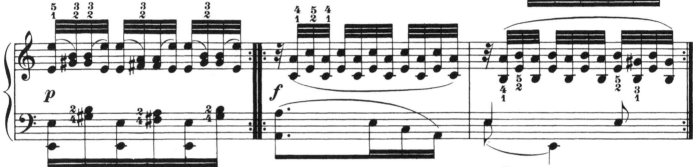

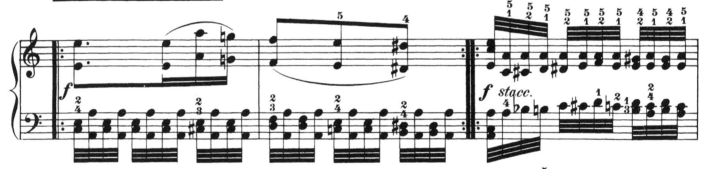

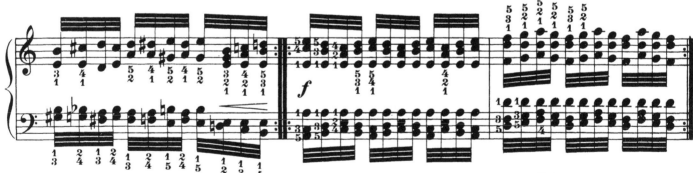

Coda.

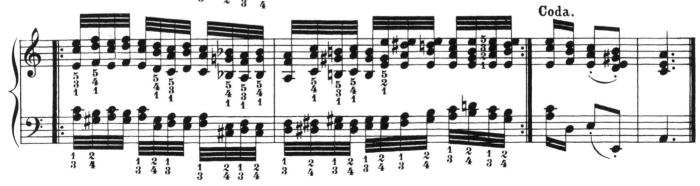

Each repeat 12 times.

Allegro moderato. (♩=96.)

19.

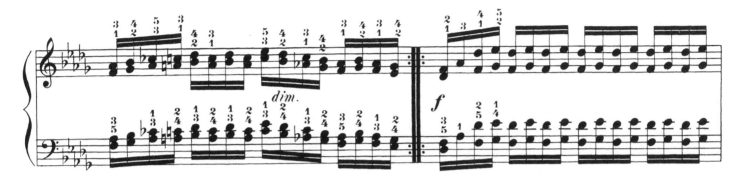

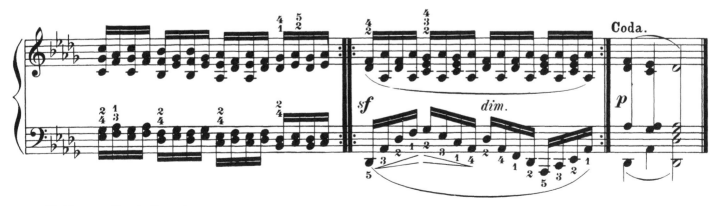

*) Also practise in D major.

13435

Each repeat 20 times.

Allegro molto. (♩=104.)

20.

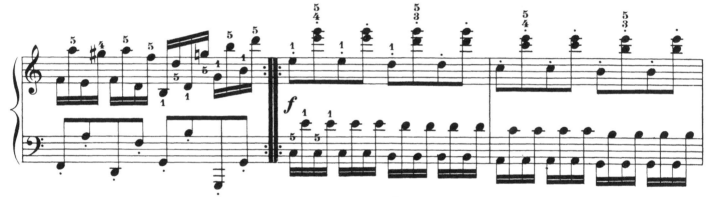

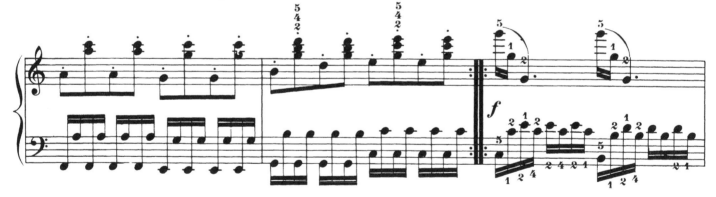

*) Also transpose a semitone higher and lower.

13435

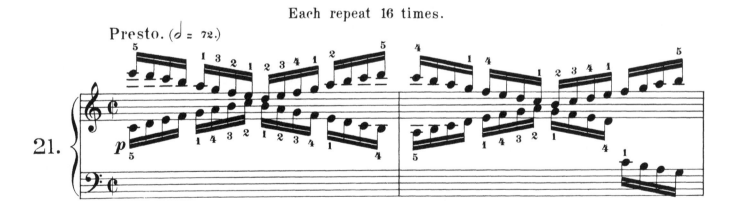

Coda.

Each repeat 16 times.

Presto. ($\flat$ = 72.)

21.

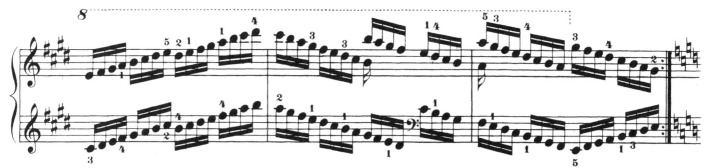

Coda.

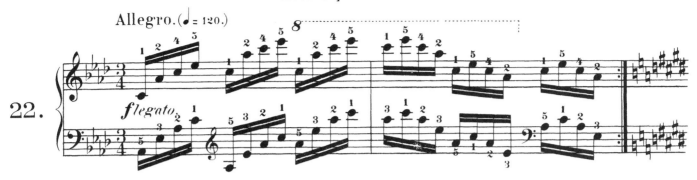

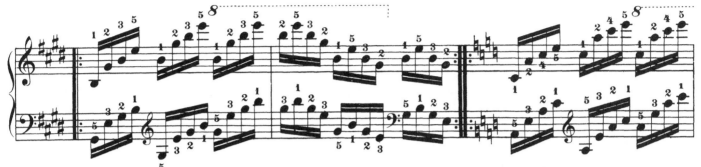

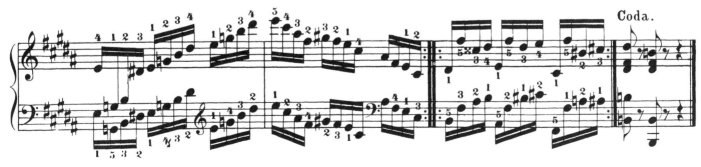

Each repeat 20 times.

Allegro vivo.($\bm{d}$ = 60.)

23.

Coda.

Each repeat 20 times.

Allegro. ($\mathbf{d}$ = 60.)

24.

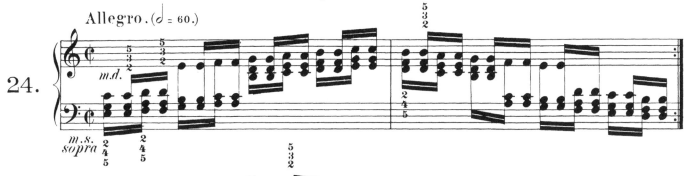

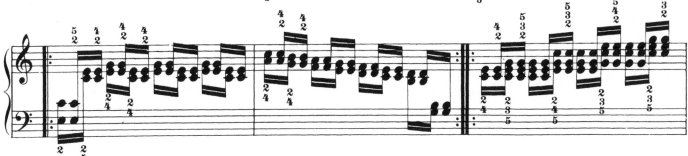

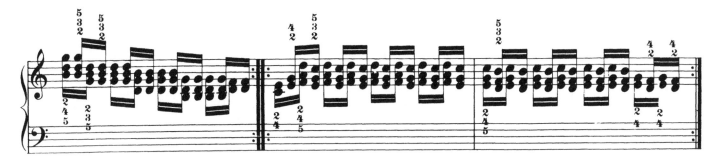

Coda.

Each repeat 10 times.

Allegro molto. ($\text{♩}_{\text{.}}$=69.)

25.

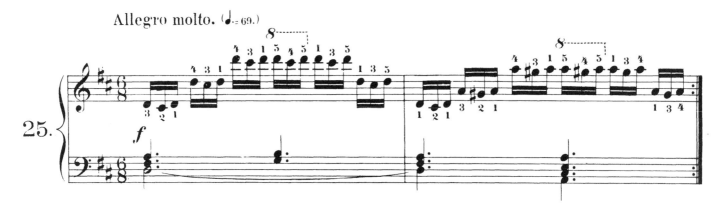

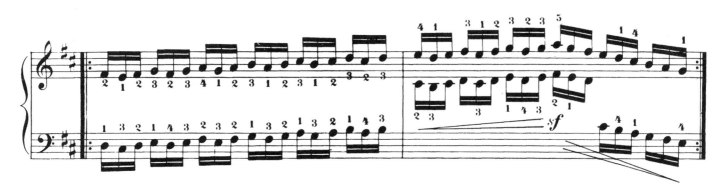

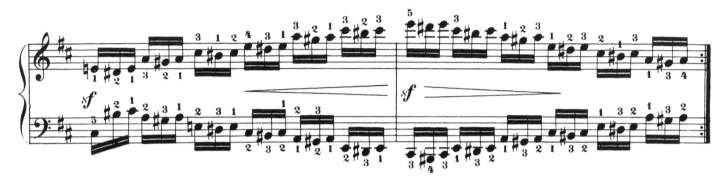

Coda.

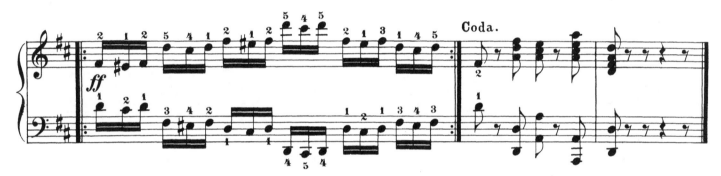

Each repeat 12 times.

Allegro. (♩ = 104.)

ten.

26.

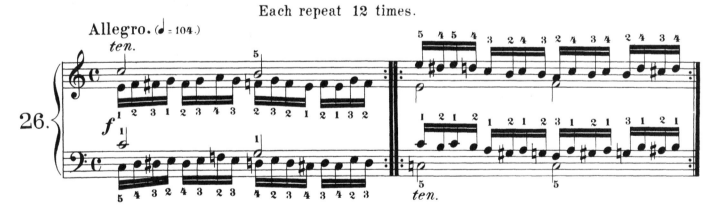

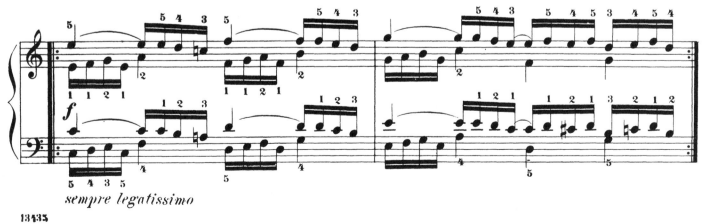

sempre legatissimo

13435

30

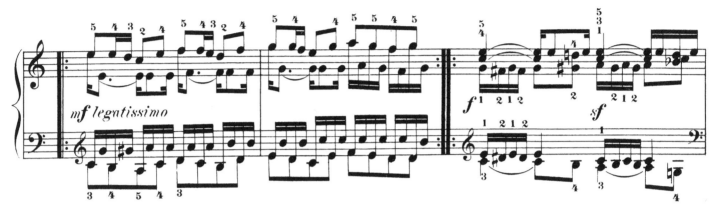

Coda.

Each repeat 20 times.

*) Also practise in D major.
3435

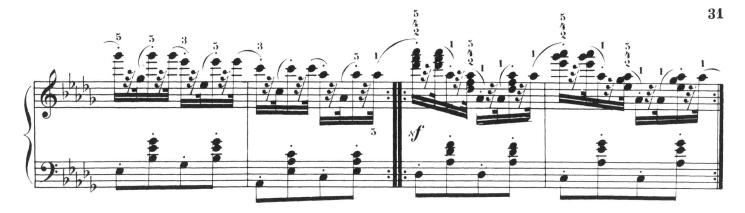

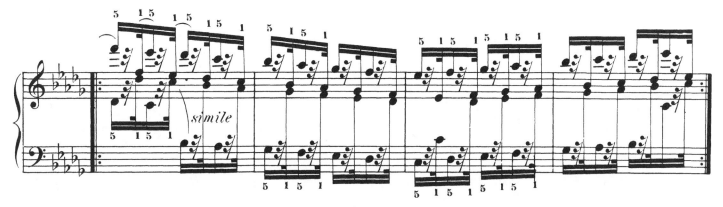

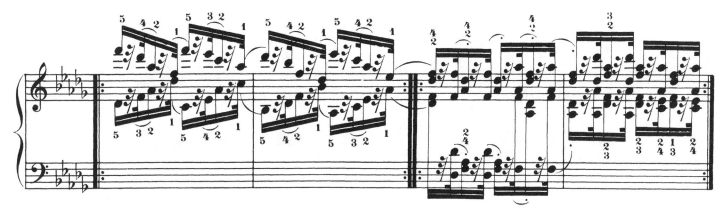

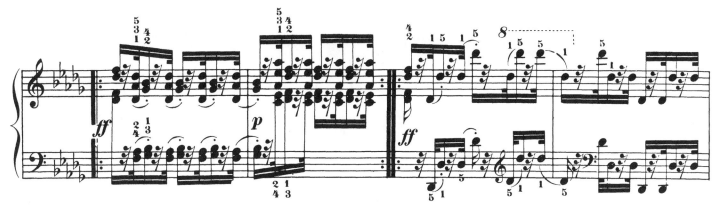

Each repeat 20 times.

28.

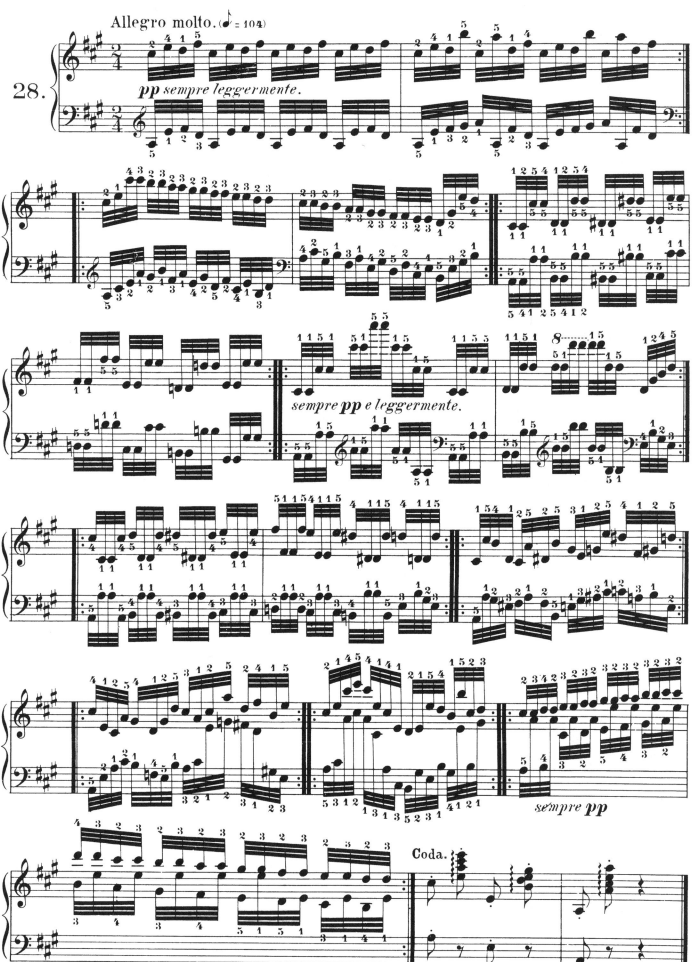

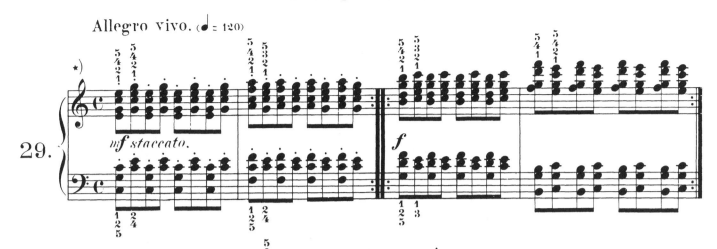

29.

Coda.

*) Also transpose a semitone higher and lower.

13435

34

Each repeat 20 times.

Velocissimo. (♩ = 112.)

30.

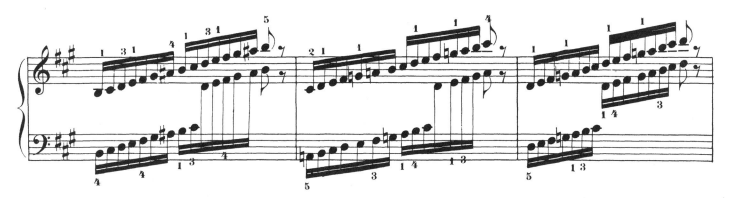

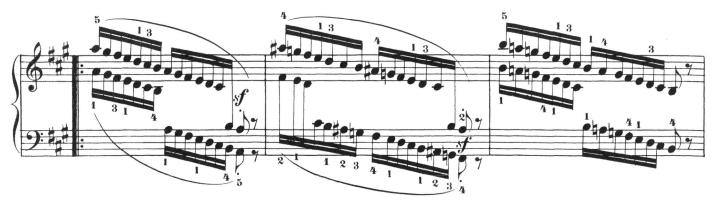

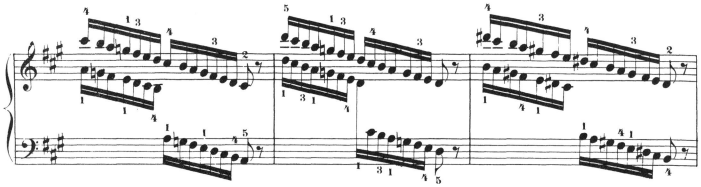

13435

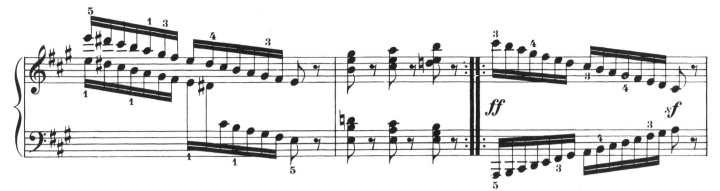

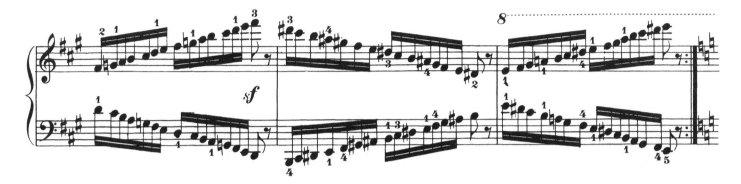

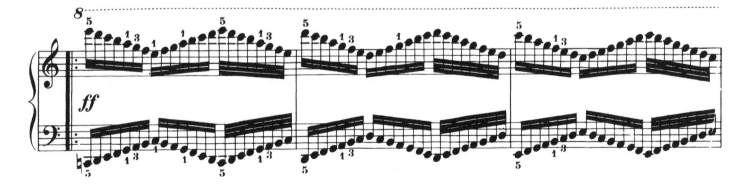

Each repeat 30 times.

31.

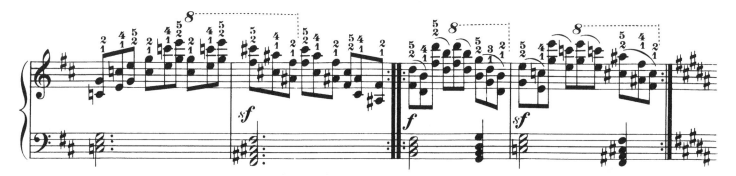

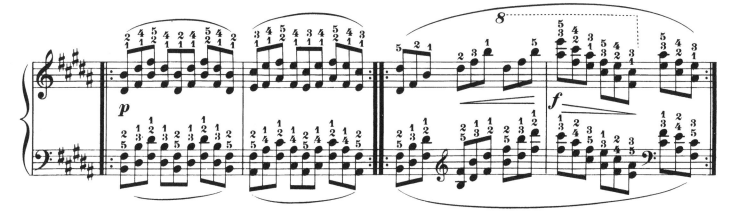

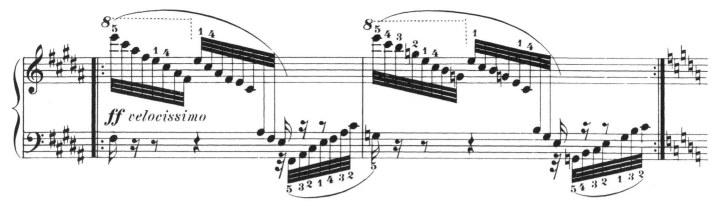

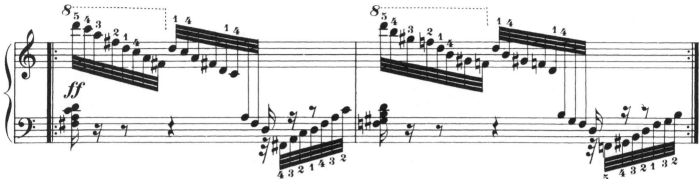

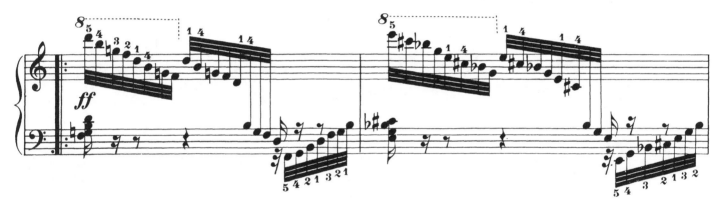

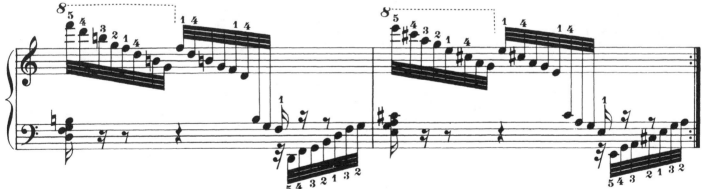

Each repeat 12 times.

Allegro molto veloce. ($\bullet$ = 88.)

32.

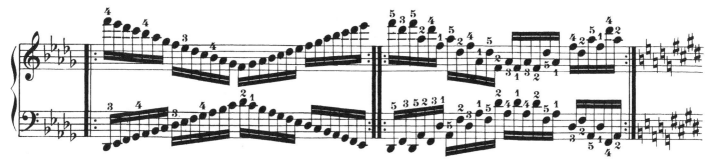

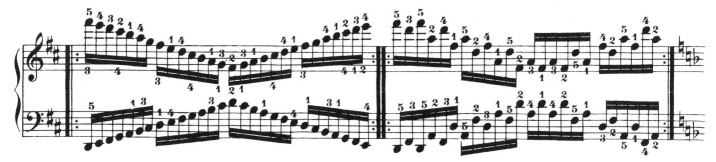

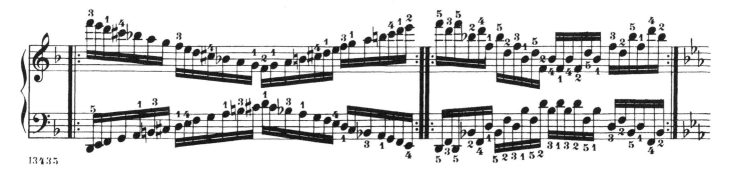

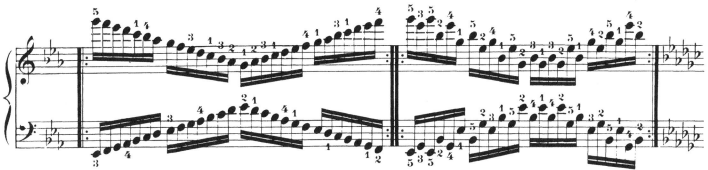

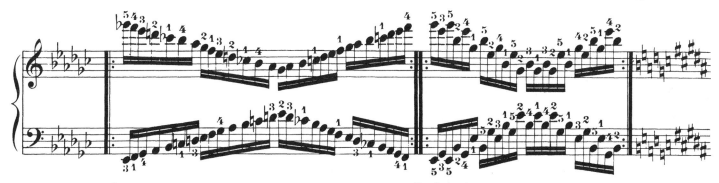

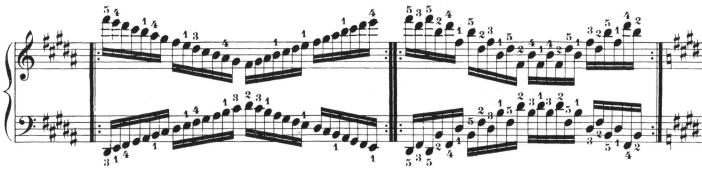

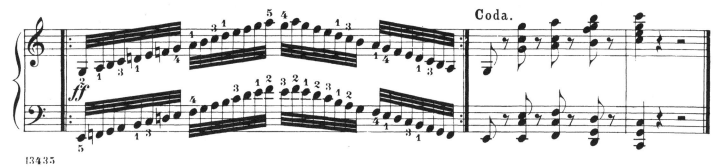

Each repeat 15 times.

Allegro. (♩ = 66)

33.

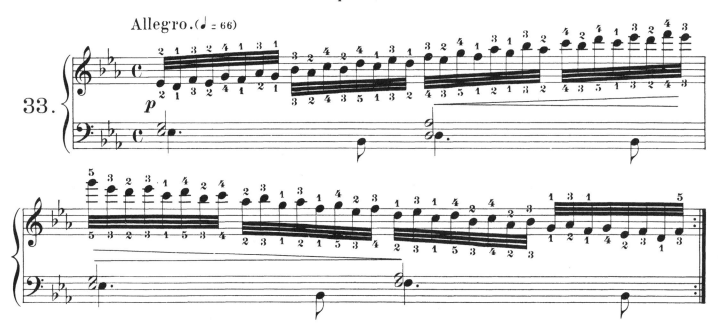

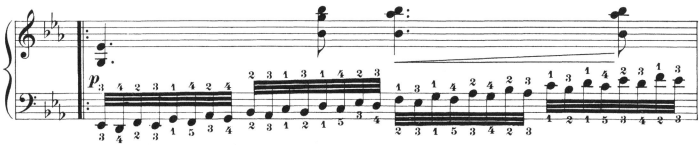

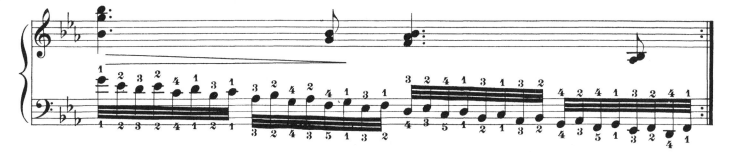

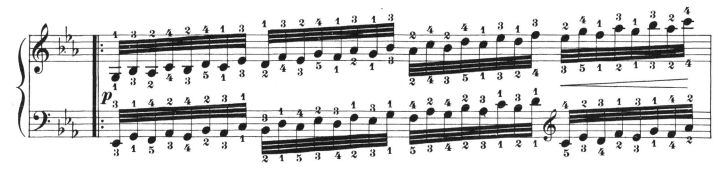

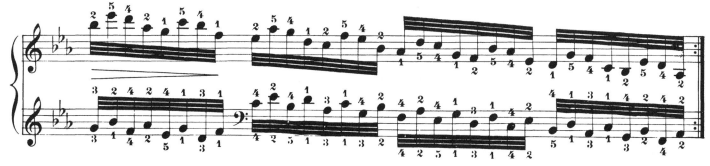

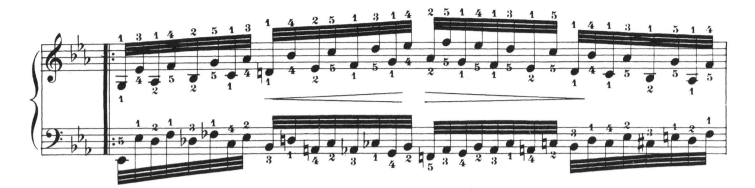

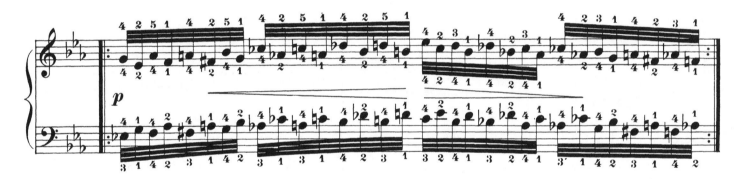

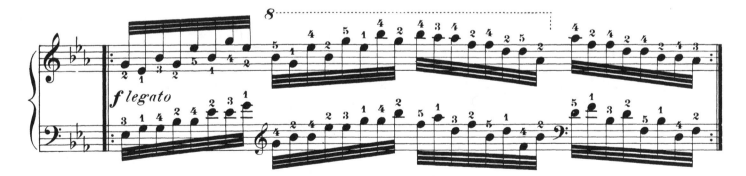

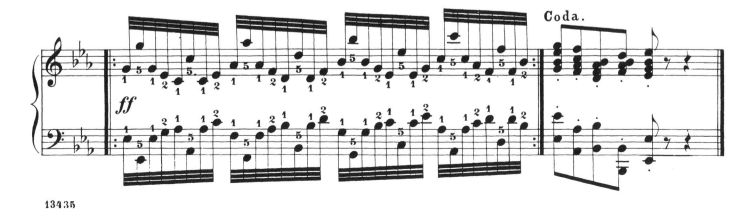

13435

Each repeat 12 times.

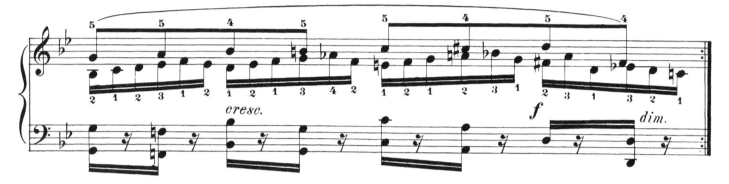

34.

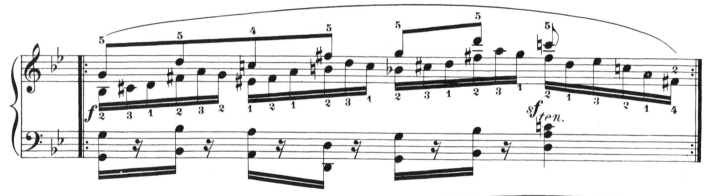

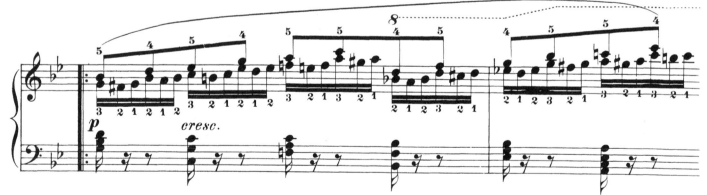

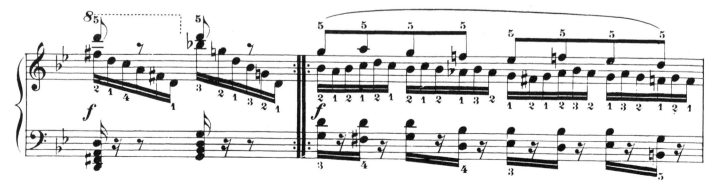

Coda.

Each repeat 16 times.

Allegro molto.($\quad$ = 66)

35.

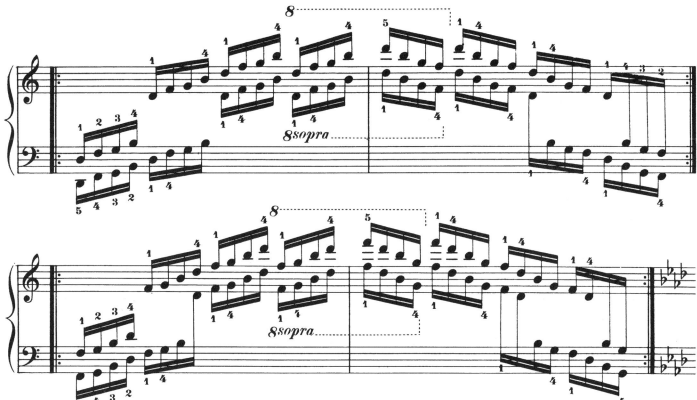

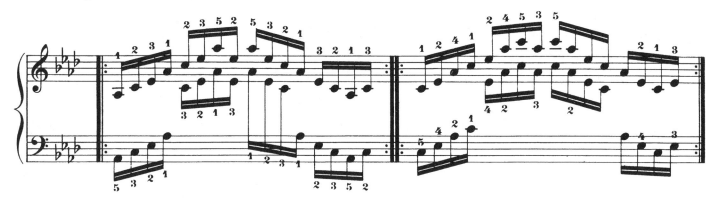

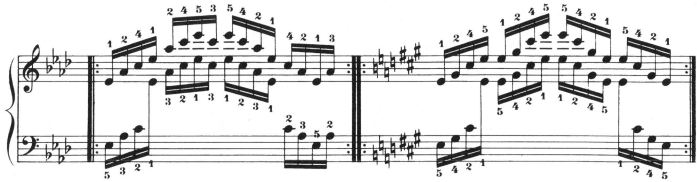

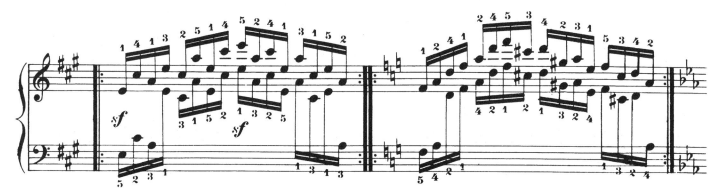

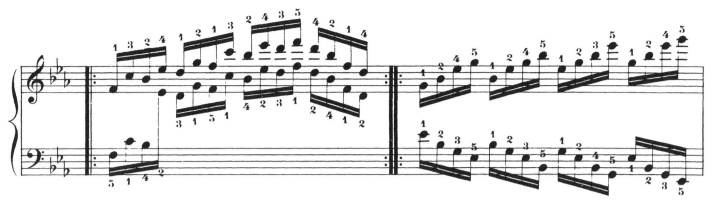

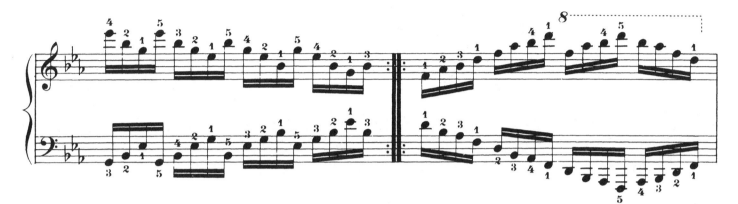

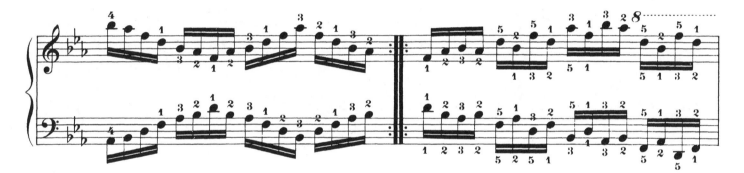

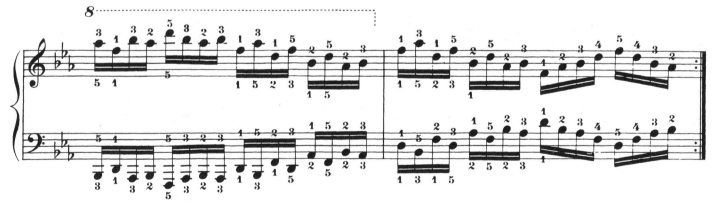

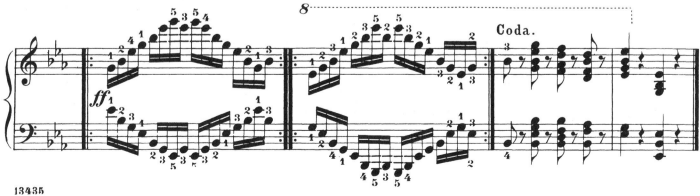

Each repeat 20 times.

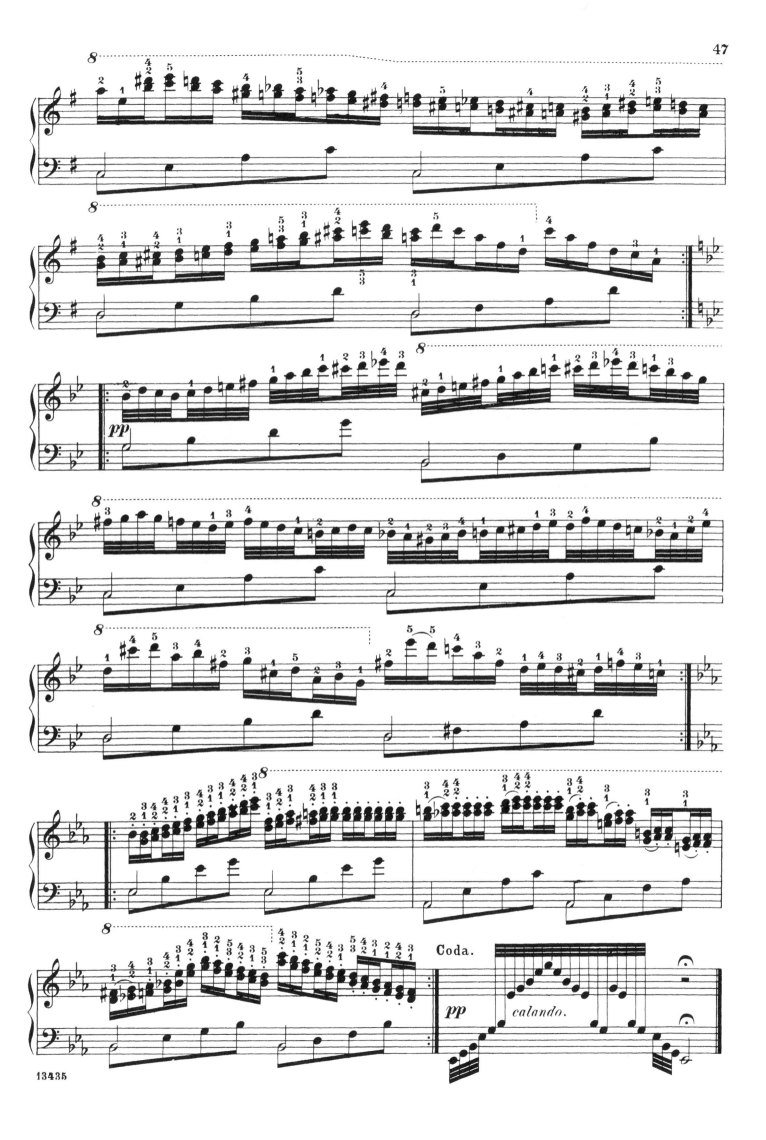

Each repeat 8 times.

37.

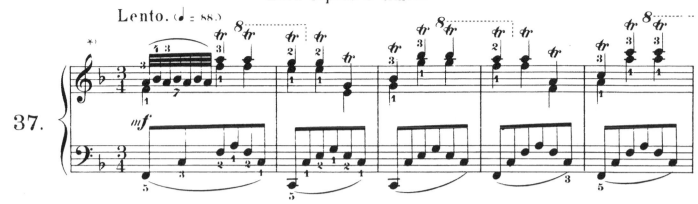

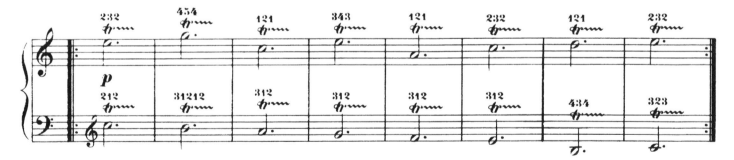

*) Also practise in F♯. with the same fingering.

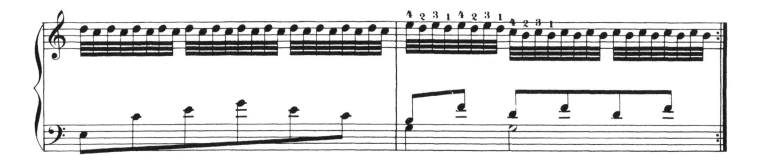

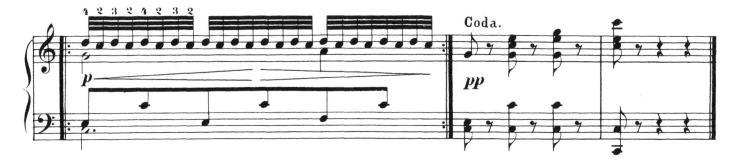

Each repeat **20** times.

Allegro moderato. ($\quad$ = 100)

38.

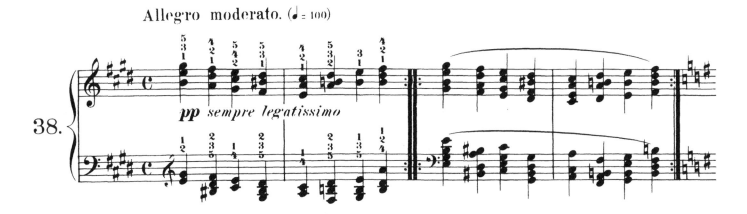

pp sempre legatissimo

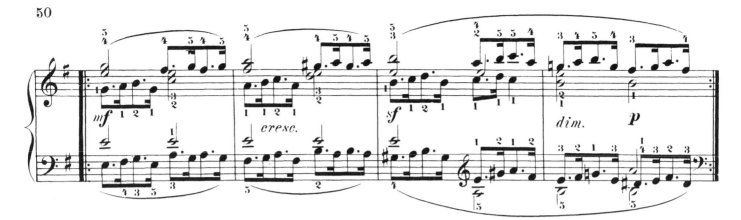

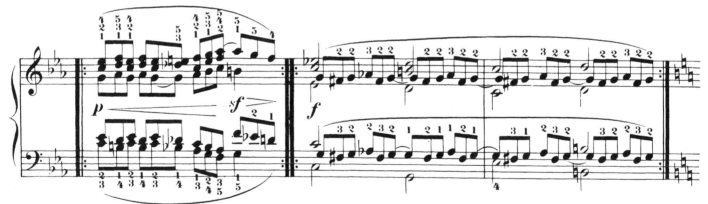

Each repeat 8 times.

Allegretto vivace. ($\bullet$ = 72)

39.

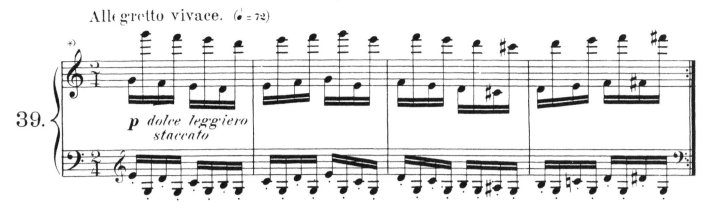

p dolce leggiero
staccato

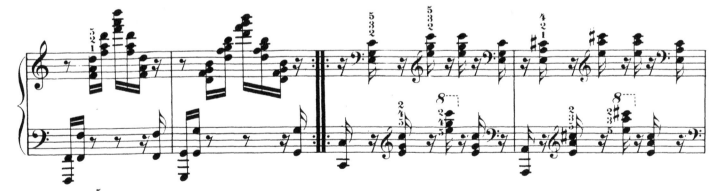

Coda.

*) Also practise in C♯.
13435

Each repeat 6 times.

40.

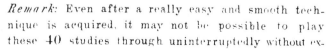

Remark: Even after a really easy and smooth technique is acquired, it may not be possible to play these 40 studies through uninterruptedly without excessive fatigue.

In such cases, the metronome may be lowered by a few degrees.